S0-DMY-678

CASPAR LEE

THE ULTIMATE
unofficial
FAN GUIDE

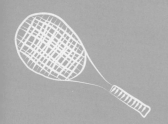

CASPAR LEE

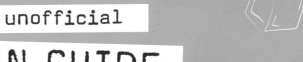
THE ULTIMATE

unofficial
FAN GUIDE

JO BERRY

Copyright © Orion 2016

The right of Jo Berry to be identified as the author of this work has been asserted in accordance with the Copyright, Designs and Patents Act 1988.

This edition first published in Great Britain in 2016 by
Orion
an imprint of the Orion Publishing Group Ltd
Carmelite House, 50 Victoria Embankment,
London EC4Y 0DZ
An Hachette UK Company

1 3 5 7 9 10 8 6 4 2

All rights reserved. Apart from any use permitted under UK copyright law, this publication may only be reproduced, stored or transmitted, in any form, or by any means, with prior permission in writing of the publishers or, in the case of reprographic production, in accordance with the terms of licences issued by the Copyright Licensing Agency.

A CIP catalogue record for this book is available from the British Library.

ISBN: 978 1 4091 6727 3

Printed in Italy

Design: Us Now

CASPAR LEE IMAGE CREDITS:

AGF s.r.l./REX/Shutterstock: page 31 (top); Broadimage/REX/Shutterstock: page 31 (bottom); David Fisher/REX/Shutterstock: page 2, 15 (top right), 17 (right), 30, 35; Getty Images: page 4, 6–7, 8 (top), 25, 39, 43, 47, 59 (right), 62 (left/ top right), 63; IBL/REX/Shutterstock: page 32; Jim Smeal/REX/Shutterstock: page 59 (bottom left); Jonathan Hordle/REX/Shutterstock: page 15 (top left), 16 (right), 50, 51, 53; Ken McKray/REX/Shutterstock: page 15 (bottom), 58; Matt Baron /BEI/Shutterstock: page 9 (top); PA Images: page 29, 62 (bottom right); LNP/REX/Shutterstock: page 14; Shutterstock/ smpics: page 8; Shutterstock/michaeljung: page 9; Shutterstock/AdrianHillman: page 12; Shutterstock/mbbirdy: page 20; Shutterstock/StrenghtOfFrame: page 21; Shutterstock/tupungato: page 21;Shutterstock/AngiePhotos: page 22; Shutterstock/johny007pan: page 22; Shutterstock/ BrettCharlton, Leontura: page 23; Shutterstock/tomgigabite: page 23; Shutterstock/leezsnow, Jitalia17, RossiAgung, SteveCash, yarn: page 37; Shutterstock/Geber86, PeopleImages, Eugenio Marongiu, pidjoe: page 40; Shutterstock/Xavier Arnau, PeskyMonkey, Michael Krinke, RealCreation, IakovKalinin, DanielPrudek: page 41; Shutterstock/ca2hill: page 42; Shutterstock/ulimi: page 43; Shutterstock/leremy: page 46; Shutterstock/vuk8691: page 47; Shutterstock/iamStudio: page 54, 55; S Meddle/TV/ REX/Shutterstock: page 16 (left); Startraks Photo/REX/Shutterstock: page 33 (bottom); Steve Bisgrove/REX/Shutterstock: page 33 (top); Variety/REX/Shutterstock: page 17 (left).

Every effort has been made to fulfil requirements with regard to reproducing copyright material. The author and publisher will be glad to rectify any omissions at the earliest opportunity.

www.orionbooks.co.uk

CONTENTS

GET TO KNOW CASP~~X~~A R

He's one of the most popular vloggers in the world, with over five millio
subscribers to his YouTube channel and more than three million follower
on Twitter. Caspar Lee is known for his funny videos, his laugh-a-minute
movie *Joe & Caspar Hit the Road* (made with friend and housemate Joe
Sugg), and, of course, for his deep love of pizza.

And he's not just a vlogger. Caspar sang as part of the YouTube boyban
for Comic Relief, acted alongside *Friends'* Lisa Kudrow in *Web Therapy*,
has performed stand-up comedy, and even provided the voice of a
seagull for the second SpongeBob SquarePants movie! Is there anything
Caspar can't do? We don't think so!

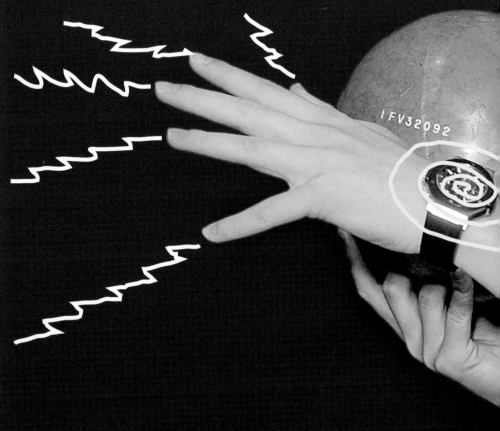

QUICK FACT DOWNLOAD

- ☐ **Full Name:** Caspar Richard George Lee
- ☐ **Date Of Birth:** 24th April 1994
- ☐ **Height:** 6ft 2in
- ☐ **Home Town:** Caspar was born in London but grew up in Knysna, South Africa
- ☐ **Favourite Animal:** Dog – Caspar had his own dog when he lived at home in South Africa
- ☐ **Thing That Annoys Him Most:** People spelling his first name wrong. It was even spelled incorrectly (Casper instead of Caspar) on the poster for *Spud 3: Learning to Fly*, his movie debut
- ☐ **Best Friend:** Josh, who was originally mean to Caspar at school, but is now his best friend and knows him better than anyone
- ☐ **Favourite Food:** Pizza – and he puts banana on it! His favourite pudding is tiramisu
- ☐ **Favourite Drink:** Gin and Tonic
- ☐ **Favourite Song:** 'Lose Yourself' by Eminem

- ☐ **Favourite Sport:** He played a lot of tennis at school and was pretty good at it – a good thing, really, as Caspar admits he is very competitive!
- ☐ **Strange Talent:** He can get his leg behind his head! Looks very painful though…
- ☐ **Odd Secret:** Caspar says he never learnt how to tell the time!
- ☐ **Star Sign:** Taurus
- ☐ **Eye Colour:** Blue
- ☐ **Hair Colour:** Brown
- ☐ **Most Embarrassing Moment:** When Caspar went to pick his phone up from a table and accidentally took Harry Styles' phone instead!
- ☐ **Proudest Moment:** Going to Uganda with Comic Relief to visit a children's hospital, and then raising £21,000 in a week with his YouTube followers
- ☐ **Celebrity Crush:** Gigi Hadid
- ☐ **The Key to Caspar's Heart:** A girl that can cook!

CASPAR'S YOUTUBE STORY

While Caspar has tried acting, stand-up comedy, singing and DJ'ing, his first love will always be YouTube. He was only 16 years old when he started his YouTube journey, and you can check out below how he went from teenager with 1000 subscribers to online megastar in just a few years…

19TH SEPTEMBER 2010
FIRST EVER VIDEO

Caspar uploaded his first video to YouTube, aged just 16. It was a video of him talking about the joys of taking a bath, and he's quite embarrassed about it now! Over the next year he uploaded more than 60 videos and reached about 1000 subscribers. Unfortunately, someone sabotaged his account and he had to start all over again with a new YouTube channel in 2011.

10TH NOVEMBER 2011
CHANGING CHANNELS

Caspar started his new channel and uploaded his first video on 22nd January 2012. This one was much more successful and Caspar credits it to luck, meeting the right people at the right time and making videos people wanted to watch.

15TH APRIL 2012
GOING LIVE

Caspar began doing live webcam shows on the website YouNow and more than 100 people tuned in. One day, a YouTuber called Sam Pepper told more than 1000 people to watch Caspar's live show and subscribe to his YouTube channel, and it got Caspar more than 100 new subscribers in one night.

3RD JUNE 2012
10,000 SUBSCRIBERS!

Caspar flew to London where he was met by new friend Jack Harries, and Caspar went on to make lots of videos with the friends he had met over the internet, including Bertie Gilbert, Alfie Deyes and Marcus Butler. On 3rd June, he posted a video commemorating 10,000 subscribers and celebrated by doing the Salt and Ice Challenge – with his mum!
(And she won!)

Fancy doing the Salt and Ice Challenge with a friend at home? Simply put a teaspoon of salt in your hand, and then hold an ice cube in the same hand. Close your hand and keep it that way for two minutes – bet you can't do it, as it really starts to hurt! See who can last the longest!

23RD OCTOBER 2012
SECOND CHANNEL

Caspar launches a second channel, MoreCaspar, featuring bloopers and outtakes from some of his YouTube videos.

2ND SEPTEMBER 2012
100,000 SUBSCRIBERS!

To celebrate the milestone of 100,000 subscribers, Caspar decided to jump out of an aeroplane! Yes, he signed up to jump from 10,000ft and looked pretty nervous boarding the plane beforehand. Caspar did a tandem jump with a qualified skydiving instructor and filmed it to thank all his fans for their support.

9TH DECEMBER 2012
300,000 SUBSCRIBERS!

How do you top jumping out of a plane? When Caspar reached 300,000 subscribers just three months later, he jumped off a bridge! Joining the Red Bull team, a very scared-looking Caspar complete with a GoPro strapped to his helmet, did a bungee jump 216 metres from Bloukrans Bridge in the Western Cape area of South Africa, which is one of the highest bungee jumps in the world. Wow.

15TH JULY 2013
1 MILLION SUBSCRIBERS!

When Caspar reached one million subscribers he posted a video in which he interviewed a handful of the people that watch him on YouTube to find out what they liked about him. And some of the responses were very strange…

According to CNN.com, these are the ten highest bungee jumps in the world – and Caspar did one of them!

1 Royal Gorge Bridge, Colorado, USA **321 metres**

2 Macau Tower, Macau, China **233 metres**

3 Verzasca Dam, Switzerland **220 metres**

4 Bloukrans Bridge, Western Cape, South Africa **216 metres**

5 Europabrücke Bridge, Innsbruck, Austria **192 metres**

6 Niouc Bridge, Val d'Anniviers, Switzerland **190 metres**

7 Altopiano di Asiago, Vicenza, Italy **175 metres**

8 Kölnbrein Dam, Austria **169 metres**

9 Vidraru Dam, Romania **166 metres**

10 The Last Resort, Bhote Koshi River, Nepal **160 metres**

22ND AUGUST 2014
2.5 MILLION SUBSCRIBERS

BBC Radio 1 announced that it would ask a series of successful YouTubers to DJ for the station; among them was Caspar, who had exceeded two and a half million subscribers by the summer of 2014.

13TH APRIL 2015
3 MILLION SUBSCRIBERS!

Caspar was in Palm Springs, California, when he reached three million subscribers. He was there for the Coachella music festival and posted a video of himself lying in the sun talking about how much he enjoyed being on YouTube and how lucky he is.

24TH AUGUST 2015
5 MILLION SUBSCRIBERS!

Reaching five million subscribers was an amazing feat for Caspar and he celebrated by posting a video featuring some of his YouTube friends, like Zoe Sugg, Joe Sugg, Maisie Williams and Alfie Deyes, saying how much they hate him! Even his mum says he nearly killed her when he was born because he had such a big head, so no wonder Caspar cries... Never mind, at least he can console himself that his channel is the 165th most subscribed on YouTube. Congratulations Caspar!

...nd now – more than 5.5 million subscribers and growing! And 1.7 million or his second channel, norecaspar...

Zoella

YOUTUBER FRIENDS

One of the reasons Caspar moved from South Africa to England was that he knew linking up with successful – and friendly – fellow YouTubers would help his own YouTube channel. Since moving to London, he's not only worked with some of the best YouTubers, he's become friends with them as well – and even lived with a couple! Here's a quick guide to Caspar's YouTube friends…

ZOE SUGG (ZOELLA280390)

Zoe Sugg is the older sister of Caspar's roommate Joe and a phenomenally successful YouTuber in her own right, better known as Zoella. With her mix of make-up tips, fashion advice and chats about her life, she has gained nearly 10 million subscribers and also written two novels – *Girl Online* and *Girl Online: On Tour*. She also appeared in the 2015 Comic Relief edition of *The Great British Bake Off* and has her own brand of make-up. Zoe has done a few videos with Caspar, including 'Advice With Caspar Lee' and 'What Guys Look For in a Girl'.

ALFIE DEYES (POINTLESSBLOG)

Alfie was Caspar's first flatmate when he moved to London, but now Alfie is back in his hometown of Brighton, where he lives with girlfriend Zoe Sugg. Alfie's YouTube channel is the Pointlessblog, featuring lots of challenges and pranks (some starring Caspar, such as the 'Blindfolded Drawing Challenge' and the 'Ghetto Booty Dance'). Alfie has also written two books that have become bestsellers.

Alfie

Jack & Finn

JACK AND FINN HARRIES (JACKSGAP)

Twins Jack and Finn run the YouTube channel JacksGap – it was originally Jack's channel that he launched in 2011 while he was taking a gap year travelling, but Finn joined in the following year. A lot of the videos were of the pair's travels in India and the Far East, but more recently the twins have focused on climate change and have posted some really interesting videos about it. In his videos, Jack had Caspar teach him how to speak South African – and how to pick up girls… using One Direction lyrics!

OLI WHITE (THEOLIWHITETV)

Oli

Comedy video maker Oli does stunt videos with his little brother and vlogs about his travels, including trips to South Africa and Thailand he took with Joe Sugg and Caspar. He and Caspar have appeared in each other's videos, such as one where they tried Filipino food, and he was the judge in the YouTuber Olympics – a contest in which Joe and Caspar attempted to do some contests, including cup stacking and aiming tennis balls at each other. Oli also appeared in Caspar and Joe's movie, *Joe & Caspar Hit The Road*.

Marcus

Jim

TYLER OAKLEY (TYLEROAKLEY)

American Tyler has over seven million subscribers to his channel, which features advice, travel guides and challenges. A huge success around the world, he's even met President Barack Obama at the White House and interviewed first lady Michelle Obama about education in the US. And he's chatted with One Direction, too! Tyler's videos with Caspar include the 'Minion Torture Challenge' and a trip with fellow YouTubers to 'Hogwarts' (the Harry Potter Warner Bros. Studio Tour outside London).

JOE WELLER (JOEWELLER)

Football fan Joe makes – you guessed it – vlogs about football, FIFA games and he even writes football songs, too. And he was foolish enough to agree to do the Naked Brain Freeze challenge with Caspar last year – not one to try at home as Joe really didn't look well at the end of it!

MARCUS BUTLER (MARCUSBUTLERTV)

Best known for his challenge videos, Marcus was a software entrepreneur before he became a full-time YouTube vlogger. Close friends with Alfie Deyes, they have done quite a few videos together, including the 'Eggs to the face' quiz. Marcus has over four million subscribers of his own and has done interviews and videos with Caspar

Tyler

Tanya

including 'The Friendship Test' (in which he and Jim Chapman tried to prove who was the better friend) and 'How To Kiss With Caspar Lee'.

JIM CHAPMAN (J1MMYB0BBA)

Jim has a degree in psychology, which probably comes in handy for the advice videos that made him popular. He also pranks his friends, does video challenges and is known for his fashion sense – he was voted the 17th Best Dressed Man in Britain by *GQ Magazine* in 2015. Jim, who is married to YouTuber Tanya Burr, has appeared in vlogs trying to teach Caspar how to grow up, and also appeared with Caspar, Alfie, Marcus and Joe as part of a YouTube spoof boyband in 2014.

TANYA BURR (PIXI2WOO)

Tanya is the ex-make-up counter girl who rose to fame making her own beauty vlogs. She has since launched her own cosmetic line, written the bestselling book *Love, Tanya*, and followed it with the 2016 cookery book *Tanya Bakes*. Tanya married Jim Chapman in September 2015 and the two often appear in each other's blogs. Tanya has also appeared in a few of Caspar's, teaching him how to talk to girls, and even quizzing him about make-up!

CASPAR'S PIZZA FACTORY

If you've watched just a few of Caspar's vlogs, you'll have already figured out that his favourite food of all time is pizza. But what are his ultimate pizzas? We're sure it's not the deep-pan oven one that he burnt in a frying pan in one of his videos…

- **Bacon and banana** – Caspar's top tip is to put the banana on first, followed by the bacon on the top. If he's feeling extra adventurous, he also adds sweet peppers.
- **Pepperoni** – sometimes the classics are the best.
- **Pizza on pizza** – in May 2015, Caspar tweeted a photo of cheese and tomato pizza… with little triangles of cheese and tomato pizza as the topping. Double pizza fun!
- **Cheese and tomato** – because a plain pizza is better than no pizza at all.
- **The biggest pizza in the world** – this one would keep Caspar busy for a few weeks. In 2012, a pizza named 'Ottavia' was made by Dovilio Nardi, Andrea Mannocchi, Marco Nardi, Matteo Nardi and Matteo Giannotte in Rome. It was 131 feet in diameter and weighed over 51,000lbs – 8,800lbs of that was cheese!

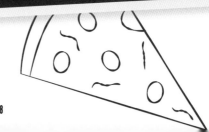

MAKE YOUR OWN PIZZA

Caspar has attempted to make pizza on South African TV (it wasn't very round!) and also with his mum (which he fed to his doll, Emma). We're sure you can do better with this simple recipe for homemade pizza:

You will need:

500g strong white bread flour, plus extra for dusting

2 tsp fast-acting yeast

2 tbsp olive oil

2 tsp salt

300ml warm water

1 tbsp tomato pasta sauce or tomato pizza sauce

½ ball of mozzarella, torn or sliced

the toppings of your choice

Method:

◼ Mix together the flour, yeast, oil, salt and water until they are combined. The easiest way to do this is in a food mixer/processor, if you have one.

◼ Knead the dough for a few minutes until it is smooth and stretchy. Oil a bowl and place the ball of dough in it and cover it with cling film. Put to one side for about 45 minutes to an hour, by which time the dough will have doubled in size.

◼ Heat the oven to 230°C (gas mark 8, 450°F). Sprinkle flour on the work surface and a rolling pin and put the dough in the middle. Shape the dough with your hands into a circle, and then roll it out using the rolling pin until it is thin. The easiest way to roll the dough is to roll in one direction, then lift the dough up and turn it so it doesn't stick to the surface, before rolling again. Keep doing this until you have the right thickness for your pizza. If this is too tricky to do with a large blob of dough, divide the dough into four smaller balls and roll each one to the thickness you want (it's easier to roll a small circle than a big one!).

◼ Sprinkle a baking sheet with flour and then place the pizza base(s) onto it.

◼ Now spread tomato sauce on the base and then add pieces of mozzarella.

◼ Place your chosen toppings on the pizza, and if you are a big fan of cheese, sprinkle some grated Cheddar or mozzarella on the top.

◼ Place in the oven and bake for 10 minutes, or until the cheese is melted and the base is lightly browned.

◼ Enjoy!

HITTING THE ROAD

Thanks to the success of his YouTube channel, Caspar has been given lots of opportunities to travel around the world. He's visited his family in South Africa, travelled to California to act, and, of course, stopped off at a few places around Europe with Joe for their movie *Joe & Caspar Hit The Road.* Here are just some of Caspar's favourite places, keep an eye out for him if you get to visit them…

LOS ANGELES

Caspar and his friends travelled to LA for VidCon, where loads of YouTubers meet each year. It was on this trip that Caspar learned it's not a good idea to travel in a onesie, as he got stopped at every security checkpoint at the airport because the security guards thought he was hiding something!

Check out these great places if you're in LA:

Santa Monica – Santa Monica has beaches, shops, restaurants and a pier complete with a big wheel.

Venice Beach – home to Muscle Beach, where all the men and women who pump iron pose on the sidewalk.

Beverly Hills – one of the wealthiest areas of LA, it's not home to many movie stars now (they mainly live in the Hollywood Hills, Bel Air and Malibu) but it is the location of shopping mecca Rodeo Drive.

Anaheim – the home of the original Disneyland! There are now two parks, Disneyland and Disneyland California Adventure, featuring rides like Radiator Springs Racers, Big Thunder Mountain Railroad and the Star Tours Star Wars ride.

Hollywood – Sunset Boulevard has cool shops and restaurants, Hollywood Boulevard is a bit seedy, but best of all is Universal Studios Hollywood theme park, which is actually a little further north in Universal City. Built around a real movie studio it has rides including Despicable Me Minion Mayhem, The Simpsons The Ride and a Jurassic Park ride, too.

ITALY

Of course Italy is going to be one of Caspar's favourite places, as it is the home of pizza! As part of his road trip with Joe, Caspar tried being a gondolier in Venice, making pizza and singing opera in Verona, and even attempted learning to drive on the way to Milan, not with great results!

If you are visiting the cities in Italy that Caspar went to, make sure you look out for:

Venice – you can ride on a gondola along the Grand Canal, walk over the famous Rialto Bridge, visit pretty St Mark's Square and marvel at the stunning Doge's Palace. And don't forget to stop for pizza and a gelato!

Verona – the setting for Shakespeare's *Romeo and Juliet,* and you can see Juliet's balcony and a statue of her (people rub it for good luck). There's also a Roman theatre and arena, Castelvecchio castle and a stunning cathedral to visit.

Milan – if you've got money, you'll spend it all at this centre of Italian designer fashion. There are cheaper things to do, though, like visit the Duomo – the third largest Christian church (only Rome's St Peter's and Seville's cathedral are bigger), the Triennale design museum and the castello Sforzesco, a castle that is home to 12 mini museums.

FRANCE

Caspar visited Cannes in the south of France as part of the movie road trip, and after landing jobs as deckhands, he and Joe got to play around and swim in the bay – not bad for a sunny day's work.

If you are lucky enough to go to the millionaires' playground that is Cannes, make sure you visit:

The Film Festival – for a few days in May, some of the most famous names in movies descend on Cannes for the annual film festival to promote their latest blockbusters. You won't get a ticket to any of the screenings but wander down to the water and

you can spot a few celebrities as they arrive on boats and
stroll along the road La Croisette.

The promenade – watch for the rich and famous all year
round from one of the cafés on this coastal walkway.

Ile Ste-Marguerite – 15 minutes from Cannes by boat
is this little island that you can explore. As well as lovely
scenery, you can visit the island's Fort Royal, the home
of the prisoner known as The Man in The Iron Mask, who
was held there for a decade from 1687. Was he the brother of King Louis XIV? The
child of an affair between Louis's wife and a servant? No one knows...

SPAIN

Caspar and Joe have explored the sights of Barcelona on the northeastern coast
of Spain, and even earned some money from drawing portraits on the streets and
appearing as human statues.

If you're in Barcelona, keep an eye out for:

La Sagrada Familia – Barcelona's most famous attraction is the basilica designed by
Antonio Gaudi. And it really is spectacular.

Montjuic Fountain – this magic fountain is flooded with different-coloured lights
after dark for a truly impressive display.

Barcelona FC – if you're a football fan you'll want to visit
Barcelona's football stadium, which includes a museum
to the sport.

Picasso Museum – Artist Picasso spent his early years in
Barcelona and this museum features work from his career.

FLORIDA

Caspar flew to Florida with Alfie in 2013, and stayed
in Orlando, visiting the theme parks, chilling out by the pool, soaking up the sun,
shopping and eating lots of cheeseburgers. Luckily their hotel had some cool
waterslides, but there are also a few waterparks in the Disney area for everyone else

to try! He went to Florida again the following year, with Zoe, Joe, Alfie, Jim and Marcus.

Here are just some of the places to check out if you're in Orlando:

Universal Orlando – there are two theme parks joined together at Universal: Universal Studios and Islands of Adventure. Islands of Adventure is the one packed with rollercoasters while the Studios has the movie-themed rides and adventures. And, of course, there's a little place that spreads over both parks called The Wizarding World of Harry Potter, which you may like, too.

DisneyWorld – you could spend your whole holiday at the Disney theme parks in Orlando – there are four main parks (Epcot, Animal Kingdom, Magic Kingdom and Hollywood Studios, as well as two waterparks (Typhoon Lagoon, Blizzard Beach) to explore.

THAILAND

In July 2015, Caspar travelled with Joe and Oli to Thailand. The guys had a great time staying in a beautiful villa, but Caspar lost his phone and Joe got bitten by loads of mosquitoes! When they were in Bangkok they had some fun, too, sitting outside at the rooftop Sky Bar (until it rained), joining in a police chase and even watching Joe munch on a scorpion from a street market.

When you are in Bangkok, make sure you visit:

The Grand Palace – one of the most famous landmarks of the city, the stunning palace was built in 1782 and includes the Temple of the Emerald Buddha (Wat Phra Kaew).

The Floating Markets – visit the floating markets where traders sell their wares from wooden boats on the water.

Wat Pho – known for the gigantic, reclining, gold Buddha statue, this temple in the old part of the city features beautiful gardens and sculptures. While you are in the area, visit the street market known as Khao San Road.

JASPAR - THE BFFS!

They've travelled around Europe together in a camper van, they share a London apartment, go on joint holidays (usually with a few extra pals along for the ride) and appear in each other's videos. Since they are so often together, fans have given Caspar and his roommate the nickname 'Jaspar'. And here are some random facts about Caspar's 'other half' – step forward Joe Sugg!

Name: Joseph Graham Sugg

Date of birth: 8th September 1991

Eye colour: blue

First Pet: Joe had snails as pets growing up!

Who he wanted to be as a kid: Indiana Jones

Famous sibling: his sister is Zoe Sugg, aka-make up and beauty YouTuber, Zoella.

Favourite sport: rugby. Joe played the sport when he was younger but had to give up when all his rugby pals grew much bigger than him and he stayed the same size!

Place of first kiss: Joe had his first kiss in a graveyard!

Secret crush: Mila Kunis

Most hated subject at school: swimming

Job before YouTube: he was a roof thatcher, which is why his YouTube name is Thatcher Joe. Joe has said that if his YouTube life stops, he'd go back to thatching. He carried on even when he had two million subscribers and people going past where he was working would stop to ask for selfies with him.

Downside of not being very tall: no one believes Joe is over 18, so he still has to carry ID to get into clubs!

How he got into YouTube: Zoe lent him her camera, laptop and equipment to get him started.

First celebrity Joe met: Simon Cowell, whom he was flown out to LA to interview.

First person Joe lived in with London: Caspar! He was looking for a roommate at the same time Joe was – it's fate.

JOE'S 5 BEST PRANKS ON CASPAR

Birthday Revenge Prank – Joe plastered posters of Caspar's face all over his bedroom, then added lots of stuff with his own face on, including a duvet cover, mousemats, and a teddy bear. It was more embarrassing the next day when a handyman came to work in Caspar's room and saw them!

Prank Week – after Caspar pretended to Joe that he didn't want to live with him anymore, Joe decided to get his revenge. This included the classic cling film over the toilet trick, hiding in Caspar's wardrobe and jumping out while he was filming, covering his room in sticky notes and waking him up while dressed as a scary clown!

No Sleep For Roommate Prank – The night before Caspar and Joe travelled to Orlando, Joe filled Caspar's room with alarm clocks to go off all through the night so he wouldn't get any sleep before the flight (and then would hopefully sleep all the way to America on the plane!).

Ultimate Balloon Prank – Joe filled Caspar's room with balloons, but they were also hiding Oli, dressed as a scary clown (Joe likes his scary clown mask), who jumped out at him.

The Box Prank – after trying a prank on Oli and Jim that involved Joe jumping out of a box to scare them, he tried it on Caspar but didn't get much of a reaction. So Joe decided to buy a few more boxes and fill the room with them. Some had Caspar's belongings in, but one was hiding Joe himself! And what Caspar didn't know was that Oli was hiding in one, too.

CASPAR AND HIS MUM

Caspar must have got his sense of fun and humour from his mum (or Mom, as he call her) Emily, who has bravely appeared in many of his videos – even joining in with some of his pranks and challenges. She is clearly very proud of her YouTuber son, and here are just some of her terrific moments, captured in Caspar's vlogs:

■ Caspar pretended he couldn't make it home to South Africa for Christmas, but secretly arrived so he could prank his poor mum. He snuck up behind her and pushed her into her pool, but she forgave Caspar as she was so pleased to see him!

■ The horrified look on Emily's face when Caspar showed her, on Skype, the nose piercing he had done in Australia is brilliant. She doesn't look at all impressed and tells him to take it out straight away, and sensibly warns his fans not to do it either. Even better – Caspar admits his mum is right and takes the nose ring out.

■ Caspar got his mum to help him prank Joe. Knowing that Joe pranked Caspar by waking him up on holiday, Emily tells Joe (who doesn't know Caspar is prompting his mum from another room) that she's worried Caspar isn't sleeping, and she tells him off! You can see poor Joe squirming! He looks so relieved when he realises it's a prank.

■ Not many mums would appear in their son's video, singing the 'Age of Aquarius' and pretending to be a sixties' hippy, but Caspar's mum does! She also beats Caspar in a slang challenge, so he has to perform a forfeit, which is to run down the street naked. Luckily it was filmed while he still lived at home in South Africa, so at least it wasn't too cold!

■ Caspar played egg roulette with his mum – you are supposed to boil 50% of the eggs you're using in the game and then break them over each other's heads, the hope being you get a boiled one, as a raw one means you get egg all over your head. Of course, Caspar changed the rules and only boiled six eggs out of 48 and marked them so he knew which were the boiled ones – funny how his poor mum ended up with broken egg all over her and he didn't. She works it out though and gets her own back!

CASPAR'S MOM'S BEST QUOTES

"Your head's too big for a nose ring!"

"You guys with your YouTube and your hashtags, you just don't get it" (she's joking)

"Caspar, stop being a wimp!"

"Caspar cleans up his own bedroom but makes a sh*tload of mess in the kitchen!"

"When he was a baby he was a little fat blob!"

"When he turned 12 years old – Oh. My. God. The wheels fell off. He wanted lots of things and if he didn't get them he would scream and shout!"

■ Caspar and his mum used lie detector machines for a test – but he gave her one that buzzed and gave her a shock every time, even when she was telling the truth. She got her own back by using the lie detector on him, though, and asking whether he had a girlfriend!

■ In 2013, Caspar phoned his mum and told her he'd got a girl pregnant. He was playing a prank, of course, but his poor mother didn't know that and was so cool about it, giving him advice and being incredibly supportive. It took four minutes for Caspar to admit he had prank-called his mum, and you can tell she's shocked when she tells him, 'Oh Caspar, don't do that again!' Hopefully Caspar learnt his lesson!

■ Emily has very bravely allowed Caspar in her kitchen, and has tried to teach him to make pizza and chicken curry, with rather mixed results (the pizza was so bad he tried to feed it to his doll, Emma). Watching Caspar try to slice a piece of raw chicken is hysterical, and we admire his mum's patience as he makes a complete hash of it!

CASPAR AND JOE'S DIZZY CHALLENGE

Here are some great challenges to try out with friends at home – although we recommend you move everything breakable out of the way first! Before you start each challenge, you need to spin around on the spot until you are dizzy – it's then surprisingly hard to do the simplest things like:

- move around the room without touching the floor – you have to get about by climbing from table to chair, etc. (you can always lay out a furniture assault course for you and your friends to try)
- see how many socks you can put on while standing up in one minute
- try to do a handstand and see who can hold it the longest
- see who can hold a yoga pose for the longest
- draw a picture of your face in less than a minute
- see who can juggle the longest without dropping anything (Caspar and Joe tried this with eggs but it's a bit messy so we'd go for foam balls or something like marshmallows instead)
- apply eye shadow and lipstick without a mirror
- see how many star jumps you can do without falling over

* Caspar and Joe also tried waxing their legs while dizzy but we don't think this is a good idea and could be quite painful!

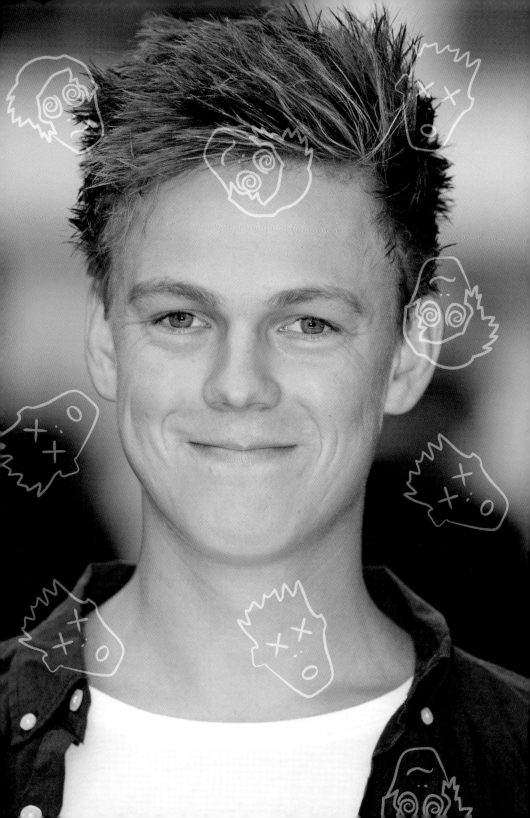

MEET CASPAR'S NEW BEST FRIENDS

Joe must be getting jealous at the growing number of famous actors Caspar is hanging out with. He's told bad jokes to Chris Pratt, played charades with Will Ferrell and even got Maisie Williams to hang out in his room. How does he do it?

MAISIE WILLIAMS

Game Of Thrones star Maisie teamed up with Caspar to offer some advice in answer to his fans' questions. The pair joked about what series of books with 'Game' in the title would be best to read, with Caspar suggesting *The Hunger Games!*

Five Facts About Maisie:

- She was 13 when she won the role of Arya Stark in *Game Of Thrones.*
- The role meant she had to leave school and have an on-set tutor. Although she's now 18, she hasn't had time yet to sit her GCSEs.
- She has over 1 million followers on Twitter and her own YouTube channel.
- She hates people who ask for her advice and then ignore it.
- When she had time off from filming *Game of Thrones,* she appeared in the spooky mini series *The Secret of Crickley Hall* and *Doctor Who.*

WILL FERRELL

Caspar interviewed Mark Wahlberg and Will Ferrell for the movie *Daddy's Home,* and Caspar got the two actors to play charades – unfortunately they didn't guess the title of *Joe & Caspar Hit The Road* from his impression!

Five Facts About Will Ferrell:

- Before he was famous he worked in a bank and as a hotel valet, where he smashed the luggage rack off a van by accidentally driving it under a low beam.
- He was the voice of the Man In The Yellow Hat in the *Curious George* movie, Megamind in the movie of the same name and President Business in *The Lego Movie.*
- He supports Celtic and Chelsea football clubs.
- He and Mark Wahlberg have appeared in two movies together, *Daddy's Home* and 2010's *The Other Guys.*
- He's 6ft 3in tall (whereas co-star Mark is only 5ft 8in)!

CHRIS PRATT

Following the success of *Guardians of the Galaxy* and *Jurassic World,* Chris Pratt is one of the biggest stars in the world, yet he agreed to pretend to be Caspar's best friend for the day… sort of!

Five Facts About Chris Pratt

- He was working in a restaurant in Maui at the age of 19 when he was discovered and cast in the horror movie *Cursed Part 3.* He was paid just $700 for his performance.

- He made his name in the teen TV dramas *Everwood* and *The OC*. On Everwood he dated actress Emily VanCamp, who played his sister.
- He's married to the actress Anna Faris and they have a three-year-old son called Jack.
- He's got a pet lizard named Puff.
- He can speak German fluently, having learnt it at school.

KEVIN HART

Comic actor Kevin Hart makes Caspar cry when he denies they're best friends, but is a pretty good sport when the pair play a best friend game and they even end up hugging. Awww…

Five Facts About Kevin Hart

- Kevin started out by winning some amateur comedy competitions in clubs near where he grew up in Philadelphia.
- He first performed using the name Lil Kev (he's only 5ft 3in tall) but it didn't always go well – he once had a piece of chicken thrown at him from the audience.
- One of his biggest movie hits is *Ride Along* with rapper/actor Ice Cube, which opened in 2013 and was followed by a sequel in 2016.
- Before he was famous, Kevin worked as a shoe salesman.
- If he could get into a tickle fight with any celebrity, he would chose *Modern Family's* Sofia Vergara.

MICA BELLUCCI AND LEA SEYDOUX

Caspar got to interview not just one, but two of the Bond girls from the movie *Spectre.* And you can see how nervous he is with both of them sitting next to him on the sofa – and they notice, too! No wonder his friend Josh says it is the worst thing he has ever seen in his life!

Five Facts About Monica and Lea

■ Italian actress Monica is fluent in Italian, English, French and Farsi.

■ Monica was 50 when she appeared in *Spectre,* making her the oldest Bond girl there has ever been.

■ Paris-born Lea wanted to be an opera singer when she was a child and studied music at the Conservatoire de Paris.

■ Both Lea and Monica were models before they began their acting careers.

■ Kissing scenes between Monica and Bond star Daniel Craig and Craig and Lea had to be cut before *Spectre* could be released in India. All the rude words in the movie were removed, too!

CASPAR'S 10 MOST ANNOYING LIST

Caspar's a pretty easygoing sort of guy, but even he gets annoyed by things (like Joe's pranks) once in a while. Here are the top ten things that really bug him:

1 Getting sunburnt

2 Stubbing your toe

3 People who say they are afraid of clowns (he's obviously forgetting all the times he has screamed when Joe has been wearing a clown mask)

6 People who read over your shoulder when you're writing something private

5 People who have their phone turned off when you need to get hold of them

4 Paper cuts

7 Smoking in public

8 People who take ages to reply to texts

9 Clingy girls

10 Girls who hardly eat or are always on a diet

WORDSEARCH

We've picked out some words associated with Caspar's life and hidden them in this wordsearch for you to find. See how quickly you can spot them, and test your friends, too! Words are hidden vertically, horizontally, diagonally, and backwards as well as forwards! Happy hunting...

S	P	O	N	G	E	B	O	B	Y	A	C	E	A	T
E	A	R	B	D	G	Y	E	S	T	H	J	N	I	H
E	M	M	A	L	E	E	A	S	E	N	R	L	G	A
K	H	G	A	N	N	A	R	E	T	I	P	V	T	T
M	O	Q	U	C	K	Y	B	S	A	M	L	S	M	C
T	P	V	K	T	A	O	W	E	E	Y	U	L	H	H
L	N	A	Y	H	B	G	D	Y	P	Y	P	M	W	E
T	R	X	L	E	M	I	A	E	Y	O	N	E	O	R
D	M	S	H	O	Y	N	K	D	S	U	S	V	D	J
C	E	B	A	D	A	O	R	E	H	T	T	I	H	O
A	J	Y	I	O	H	T	C	I	Y	U	A	B	R	E
S	G	P	W	R	Z	T	O	F	A	B	T	J	Y	D
P	I	Z	Z	A	N	S	A	L	E	E	E	S	P	C
A	Y	I	O	C	J	L	G	A	B	H	R	K	T	E
R	A	B	S	O	U	T	H	A	F	R	I	C	A	Y

Pizza	Hit The Road	Prank	Caspar
Thatcher Joe	SpongeBob	YouTube	Emma Lee
Theodora	South Africa	Alfie Deyes	Best Mum

CASPAR LEE STYLE

Having grown up in warm and sunny South Africa, Caspar is much more comfortable in a T-shirt and shorts than the sweaters and coats he needs for a London winter! In fact, to get Caspar's look, all you need is a selection of plain T-shirts (maybe one or two with a slogan or logo on the front), board shorts and jeans. (And if you live in England, you'll probably want to turn the heating on or wear a hoodie as well.)

Or, of course, you could choose something from Caspar's own official clothing range, which he launched in September 2015. He got a load of his friends, including Adrian, Kyomi and Oli, to help out by modelling the t-shirts and hoodies with 'Caspar Lee' on the front for his video, and the photos from their shoot are at the website for his clothes: www.casperleeclothing.com.

CASPAR'S RANDOM ACTS OF KINDNESS

Caspar's YouTube videos aren't all mad pranks and jokes, he's done lots of cute vlogs cheering up complete strangers, too. Here are just some of the random acts of kindness Caspar has tried:

❶ Taking selfies with strangers – Caspar took photos with complete strangers in Trafalgar Square in London, although one couple ran away when they saw him!

❷ Telling strangers they're beautiful – in 2014, he chatted to strangers and told them they were beautiful in Green Park in London. One man thought he was joking, but most people really appreciated the compliment!

❸ Smiling with strangers – for his birthday in 2015, he tried to take more selfies with strangers, trying to get them to smile. Lots of people joined in, but we are a bit worried about the red-faced, panting jogger!

❹ Making strangers happy – Caspar hung around a London park trying to get people to smile by saying hello and even trying to get them to sing along with him! He even held up a sign offering free hugs and got a few takers.

❺ Pizza! – Caspar met fans in Leicester Square in London and bought a few of them pizza in the summer of 2014.

10 PEOPLE CASPAR HATES ON INSTAGRAM

With millions of followers on Instagram, Caspar knows the photo-sharing site really well and has his own opinions about what you shouldn't post there. In the spring of 2015 he posted a vlog about the 10 types of people he hates on Instagram (even though some of their traits appear in his own Instagram photos!) – how many of these are you guilty of? We won't tell...

The Foodie Caspar isn't fond of those people who fill their Instagram feeds with photos of their breakfasts, lunches and dinners. Do they ever actually eat the food before it gets cold? And why do we want to see a photo of their artfully-placed fish fingers and mushy peas? Tip – if it isn't the world's biggest pizza, most expensive burger, or most calorific ice cream sundae, we don't need to see it.

The Selfie Guy That guy who seems to only take close-ups of his own face, contorted into every possible expression he can manage. Hey, put up a photo with someone else in it for a change, yeah?

The Gym Rat Feel guilty for over-eating and lounging on the sofa last week? Don't look at the gym rat's feed as it will be filled with selfies of his/her rippling physique, taut muscles and shots of them posing on gym machines in designer sportswear drinking designer water and flaunting just a little bit of – presumably – designer sweat. Pass us a cream cake...

The Show Off That person who instagrams photos of everything he owns, borrows or even stands next to. See that sports car parked on the street? See that idiot with a camera phone taking a photo of himself next to it? That's a show-off. (Pretending the car is actually his, even though he doesn't possess a driving licence? That's an idiot...)

The World Traveller Oh, aren't you lucky to go to all those interesting places around the world. Yes, please do post photos of your feet in the white sands of the Bahamas so I can look at them while I am at my desk in wet and soggy Birmingham. Thank you so much. *sobs *

#tbt Guy The 'Throwback Thursday' instagrammer obviously preferred life back when they were a kid, as all they post are throwback photos to their childhood. Awww. That photo of your sixth birthday party when you dressed up as a fluffy bunny is cute if you're TBT's parents, not very interesting if you're not.

The Artsy Guy You know that friend who thinks every photo they take is a work of art because they used a 'proper' camera rather than the one on their smartphone? That guy. And no, just because you used a sepia tint it doesn't make that photo of a festival Portaloo any more exciting.

Animal Guy Caspar doesn't like people who fill their Instagram feeds with photos of their cutesy wutesy little puppy wuppy. But shhh, we do…

Quote Guy Those people who upload meaningful quotes and place them on a pretty photo of a mountain for maximum impact. Just stop it. Stop it now.

The Photo Thief Caspar's most hated Instagrammer of all, and who can blame him. The Photo Thief combs Google Images for cool photos, often taken by professional photographers, and passes them off as his own. No, of course we don't believe you climbed Everest on your weekend off to get that awesome 'top of the world' photo. Unfollow!

THE CINNAMON CHALLENGE

You may like a little bit of cinnamon in your apple pie, but have you ever tried to eat a whole mouthful?

The challenge is for you and a friend to have a teaspoon of cinnamon each and put it in your mouth. Can you swallow it? And who will be the first to spit it out?

It's a good idea to have a glass of water handy, as it not only tastes funny, it makes your mouth feel horrible!

You can carry this challenge on by trying some other spices or odd-tasting foods. Caspar has tried the Ghost Pepper – believed to be the hottest chilli in the world, but any small chilli will do (the smaller the pepper, the hotter it is).

Why not do what Caspar did and try this challenge with a friend – melt some chocolate, and then coat a strawberry, a nut and another piece of fruit in the chocolate, and the chilli as well. That way you won't know which one is which when you try them! Unfortunately for Caspar, he got the chilli first!

For any challenges involving spicy food, make sure you have lots of water and milk to hand as it can help to drink it after something hot!

CASPAR'S GUIDE TO LOVE

Caspar has had his share of heartbreak, splitting up with two girlfriends since he has become a YouTuber, so he's pretty experienced when it comes to love and romance. Here are just some of his tips about dating and relationships:

BE YOURSELF

Caspar's a naturally funny guy and his humour has often worked when it comes to talking to girls. He tried picking up girls while speaking in funny accents and managed to get a few phone numbers from girls who got the giggles. He's also impressed a few with his kindness (giving out free hugs in a London park – awww!).

FIND SOMEONE WHO LIKES WHAT YOU DO

We don't think Caspar could date anyone who didn't like 5 Seconds of Summer, One Direction, Fridays and pizza! You don't have to like all the same things, that could get boring, but it does help if you have a few things in common.

WHAT TO WEAR ON A DATE

Caspar recommends spending time on your appearance before you go on a date – when he and Joe practised getting ready, poor Joe ended up with very gelled hair! But at least he was wearing a smart shirt. Caspar also got some dating advice from Zoe, and she sensibly suggested checking you haven't got food between your teeth and that you look generally presentable before leaving the house. Don't go overboard, just wear something nice that doesn't look like you've slept in it!

HOW TO AVOID AWKWARD SILENCES

On your date, it's worth having a few things in mind that you can talk about. Caspar suggests complimenting your date. Also, don't just talk about yourself and what you are interested in, make sure you ask your date some questions about what they like to do, too.

HAVE FUN AND DO SOMETHING INTERESTING

As Zoe points out to Caspar, playing on the Xbox is not a date! You don't have to go overboard to impress someone by spending a month's salary on the most expensive restaurant in town – often something simple works just as well. Take your date to the movies and then for food after so you get the chance to talk, or visit the local zoo so you can both laugh at the animals. Check your local paper for fun, inexpensive things to do near you – for example, in London some of the museums have a date night where you can go round the museum after hours and there's music and drinks, too.

DON'T BE TOO FULL ON

You've had your first night out – now don't bombard your date with texts and messages – you may scare them off! Don't stalk them, either! It's fine to message them the next day if the date went really well to arrange to meet up again, but if you don't get a reply, don't send message after message. You'll just come off as needy and even a little bit scary!

IF IT GOES WELL

If your date replies to your message, suggest getting together again. Now you're more comfortable with each other you can spend the time really getting to know each other and having fun. Just relax and have a good time.

IF IT'S NOT WORKING

You may have a few dates and decide it's not working. Don't stay with someone if you're miserable as you'll both end up unhappy. When it's time to break up, don't be horrible to your date, just let them down gently and explain that you're not ready for a relationship, rather than blaming it on them. Remember, always treat someone the way you would like to be treated – be nice, be kind!

TOP 10 CASPAR MOMENTS

Caspar's vlogs are filled with funny moments, cool pranks, random silliness and interesting stuff, too. Here are just 10 of his best moments – so far – on screen...

1

Falling off a gondola in Venice. And falling off a yacht in the South of France. (From Joe & Caspar Hit the Road.)

2

Screaming like a baby while trying to complete the brain freeze challenge in an ice bath.

4

Jumping out of a plane as a tandem skydiver to celebrate 100,000 subscribers.

3

Surprising his mum for Christmas by arriving in South Africa without her knowing, jumping out and pushing her into her pool!

5

Attempting to make a pizza for South African TV. Attempting to make a pizza with his mum. Attempting to make a pizza in Verona. (And failing all three times.)

6
Launching his own clothing line.

7
Blushing furiously while interviewing Bond girls Lea Seydoux and Monica Bellucci.

8
Giving Josh the best birthday surprise ever.

9
Singing really, really badly in public (in Leicester Square in London).

10
Visiting a hospital in Uganda before his 21st birthday to raise money for Comic Relief. He's already exceeded his goal of raising £21,000.

CASPAR DOES STAND-UP

After Caspar got three million followers on YouTube, he decided to face up to his biggest fear – performing stand-up comedy. He learned how to perform over the course of a week with the help of comics Russell Kane and Katherine Ryan, but – thanks to Joe dragging him off to the Isle of Wight music festival for a few days – Caspar only had one day to actually write jokes and practise performing them. He didn't do a bad job, though, and here are some of his best lines:

'I'm Caspar, from South Africa. Mum and Dad, when your son grows up in a country with years of racial division and aggression, a country in which the white people locked up Nelson Mandela, it's not a good idea to name your son after the whitest cartoon character in existence!'

HA HA HA

"None of you probably know who I am. I am Brad and Angelina's first adopted son from South Africa – it fell through when they found out I was white."

"I am a YouTuber – for you old people, that does not mean I was conceived by IVF."

"I had a maths teacher who said, "why don't you spend less time on Twitter, and more time following real people in real life?" So I followed her daughter home and got arrested."

THE 1-MINUTE SPOT THE

You have 60 seconds to spot the five differences between these two pictures.

Go
Go Go!

DIFFERENCE CHALLENGE

See page 64 for answers

ROOMMATE PRANKS

We feel a bit sorry for roommate Joe Sugg, as he seems to be on the receiving end of quite a few of Caspar's pranks! He has managed to get Caspar back a few times, though – so if you try out the following prank on your friend, brother or mum, do be prepared that they may just prank you back!

SHOWER PRANK: Caspar decided to hit Joe where it hurts – pranking him during his precious shower time. If you are feeling really mean, there are all sorts of tricks you can use to ruin your friend's shower, such as these:

❶ Caspar took Joe's red towel and sprinkled red liquid food dye on it, so when Joe dried himself the dye would come off on his body. Make sure you only use food dye, which washes off clothes and skin easily – and maybe a red colour isn't the best idea as your poor mate may panic thinking they are bleeding!

❷ If you have more than one bathroom at home, you may find that turning on the hot water in one makes the water in the other go cold. Caspar knew that if he ran his hot water, the water in Joe's shower would be freezing. Best to try this one when your poor victim is already in the shower and then run for your life as they won't be happy!

❸ Another mean one – Caspar removed Joe's showerhead and filled it with green food dye before replacing it, so when Joe started to shower he would be covered in green water. Luckily it didn't quite work as the dye came out in one lump! We don't recommend you try this one at home as you could get dye absolutely everywhere and end up having to clean it up. And your dad might not want to go to work looking like the Incredible Hulk.

❹ Caspar also filled the floor of Joe's shower with a mixture of bicarbonate of soda and vinegar, which turned into a bubbling mess. And it smelt really bad, too! Again, the prank may be on you by the end, as you'll have to scrub it all up.

ULTIMATE CASPAR HAIR – GET THE LOOK

Caspar is known for his distinctive spiky haircut, and it's not too tricky to create the look for yourself. Just follow our quick instructions:

You will need:

Styling gel and/or mousse

Hairdryer

Round hairbrush

Comb

■ Wash and condition your hair as normal.

■ Towel-dry your hair.

■ Apply a small amount of styling gel or mousse throughout your hair and comb through.

■ Using a round brush to help guide your hair, blow-dry the back of your hair straight down.

■ Then blow-dry the sides towards the back.

■ Caspar's hair is short at the back and sides, and longer on the top. If your hair is longer than his, you can still get the look by using some gel on the sides to flatten your hair and position it going backwards.

■ Blow-dry the top of your hair by holding your head upside down and blow-drying roughly using your fingers to guide the hair back and slightly to one side.

■ Once your hair is dry, apply a little more gel to guide the front of your hair up and to the side. Don't use too much, though! You want it to look as natural as possible, not sticky and rigid. Just a pea-sized amount will do, then ruffle the hair with your hands to give it that tousled look. **There you have it - the perfect Caspar quiff!**

INSIDE CASPAR'S HOUSE

Caspar and Joe got a new apartment together in April 2014, and it's as cool as you'd expect. The two YouTubers have their own bedrooms – Casper is very jealous that Joe's has an ensuite bathroom and his doesn't – and lots of space for them to film their videos and have friends round for pizza. Take the tour and get the look:

Bedroom Caspar's bedroom is simply decorated and – when it isn't covered with his discarded clothes – he has a sleek wooden double bed in the middle, plus a matching wardrobe and chest of drawers. To get the look, try to tidy as many things out of sight as possible. Pick a cool art print to frame and hang over your bed, and choose a simple duvet cover to finish off the minimal look – Caspar goes for blue or grey, usually with stripes.

Joe's Room Like Caspar's room, Joe's is pretty minimalist and (he says) always tidier than Caspar's. He's got a desk in there, too, with his computer, and a movie clapperboard propped on the windowsill.

Bathroom Caspar's bathroom – which is the one every visitor to his home gets to use, so he has to keep it neat – is dark grey tile with a few navy accessories. If you want to clear the clutter from your bathroom, most supermarkets sell soap dispensers, toothbrush holders and other matching accessories quite cheaply.

Harry Potter's Room Yes, the boys have a cupboard under the stairs that they pretend is for Harry Potter. We actually think it's where Caspar keeps his doll Emma when she isn't on camera.

Dining Room Caspar and Joe have a living area that is a dining room, living room and kitchen. The dining part has a wooden table and cream chairs – and a surprisingly feminine blue flower vase on it. Do we think that was Caspar's mum's?

Living Room The white living room, with black and white chairs, is dominated, of course, by their flat-screen TV and collection of DVDs and games. They've got a shaggy grey rug and glass table in the centre, while Caspar's 'office' – his desk, chair and computer – is off to one side. Want the look for your room? Go for black, white or grey accessories but make sure there are some soft touches (rugs, cushions, etc.) about so it doesn't look too harsh.

Kitchen Caspar and Joe's kitchen is, surprise surprise, black, but they have softened it up a bit with wood worktops and even an orchid on the counter. Wonder which one of them remembers to water it? (We think it'll be Joe.) There is an oven, but we doubt it is used for anything but warming pizza!

Want your room to look like Caspar's? You will need to:

■ Pick a neutral colour scheme – Caspar uses grey, white, black and dark blue in his home, but you could go for cream with different shades of brown.

■ Get everything as cleared away as possible – if you have a lot of books, DVDs and games, choose white or metal storage units or shelves to get everything out of the way.

■ Soften your neutral scheme with some fabrics – your duvet cover, cushions, a soft rug – maybe even a plant!

■ Keep the walls pretty bare, apart from one framed picture. You could choose an art print or favourite photo. And if you are a vinyl fan, lots of shops now sell 12-inch square frames so you can put one of your favourite album covers on the wall.

CASPAR TRUE OR FALSE

So you think you know everything there is to know about Caspar Lee?
Well, here are some statements about him and his life. Check your
answers on page 64 and find out how much of a Caspar fan you really are!

1. Caspar's first YouTube video featured him in the bath talking about
   whether bathing was better than showering.

   True: ☐   False: ☐

2. He has a doll named Mary that he calls his daughter in videos.

   True: ☐   False: ☐

3. *Game of Thrones* star Maisie Williams says it is because of Caspar's
   help that she set up her own YouTube channel.

   True: ☐   False: ☐

4. He voiced 'Seagull number two' in *The SpongeBob Movie:
   Sponge Out of Water.*

   True: ☐   False: ☐

5. One of his old YouTube channels, DiCasp, stood for the Diary of Caspar.

   True: ☐   False: ☐

6. His mum put him in an all-boys school in Durban, South Africa, because
   she was worried he would be distracted by girls.

   True: ☐   False: ☐

7. Joe Sugg has been Caspar's flatmate since he moved from South Africa
   to England in 2012.

   True: ☐   False: ☐

8. He's never broken any bones in his body.   True: [　]   **False:** [　]

9. Caspar's mum used to own a chocolate factory and he would climb into the machines filled with chocolate.

True: [　]   **False:** [　]

10. If he could have any superpower, Caspar would want to be able to fly like Superman.

True: [　]   **False:** [　]

11. Caspar's mum named him after *Casper The Friendly Ghost*.

True: [　]   **False:** [　]

12. When Caspar was little, his sister made him drink Marmite by telling him it was a milkshake.

True: [　]   **False:** [　]

13. Caspar's South African hometown of Knysna is famous for its yearly Oyster Festival, where over 20,000 of them are eaten over 10 days.

True: [　]   **False:** [　]

14. In *Joe & Caspar Hit The Road*, the boys tour Europe in a double-decker bus.

True: [　]   **False:** [　]

15. The fruit Caspar likes on his pizzas is pineapple.

True: [　]   **False:** [　]

ON THE RED CARPET

Caspar's not only a YouTube star, he's an actor, too, and has even been lucky enough to walk down his own movie star red carpet at the premiere of his and Joe's road movie, *Joe & Caspar Hit The Road.*

His first big break was winning a role in the South African movie *Spud 3: Learning to Fly,* alongside vlogger and actor Troye Sivan (as Spud) and comedy legend John Cleese. The movie began filming in the summer of 2013, and Caspar joined the cast as Garlic, a new pupil from Malawi at the 1990s boys' school Spud attends.

'He has an amazing ability as an entertainer, so to have him come in as a new element has been very exciting,' said director John Barker about casting Caspar.

'This is my first movie and my first acting gig,' Caspar added in a behind-the-scenes interview for the movie. *'The only acting I had done before was at school and I don't think my drama teacher would have imagined I would have been in a movie six months after leaving school!'*

Unfortunately the film was only released in South Africa and Australia, but it is available on DVD and online.

Caspar then appeared as himself (sort of) in *Friends'* star Lisa Kudrow's online series *Web Therapy* in 2014 and followed that with a voice role alongside roommate Joe in the animated comedy *The SpongeBob Movie: Sponge Out of Water,* with Alan Carr, though he wasn't that impressed that the seagull Joe voiced had a name (Kyle) whereas Caspar's was just known as 'Seagull no.2'. They did get to sing the theme tune, though!

Of course, the biggest movie for Caspar has been *Joe & Caspar Hit The Road.* They had a premiere in London's Leicester Square, hosted by pal Jim Chapman, and the pair made their entrance by arriving on the red carpet in the VW van from the movie. Caspar even wore black tie for the occasion, and the event was live-streamed for all their fans. They walked the red carpet, took selfies with fans and were joined by pals Josh, Marcus, Louise, Oli, Zoe, Alfie and Tanya.

'This is ridiculous! Thank you guys,' Caspar said from the red carpet, clearly stunned by all the fans that turned out. 'This would not be possible without you guys watching our videos, thank you so much,' Joe added. How sweet are they?

Up next, Caspar has a lead role in the comedy *Laid in America,* in which two foreign exchange students are kidnapped during their quest to get laid on their last night in America. He stars with Olajide Olatunji – otherwise known as YouTuber KSI – in the movie, which is due for release in 2016. You can find out more about the movie on Facebook (www.facebook.com/LaidinAmerica)

THE ULTIMATE CASPAR QUIZ

Think you know everything there is to know about Caspar Lee? Then take the quiz below and find out just how much you really know about our favourite vlogger...

Answers on page 64.

1. **What did Caspar wear when he took the brain freeze challenge, sitting in an icy bath and answering questions?**
   a) an inflatable ring
   b) arm bands
   c) swimming goggles
   d) a woolly hat

2. **What was the birthday surprise Caspar gave his friend Josh in 2015?**
   a) a trip to Los Angeles to meet Will Ferrell
   b) a free dinner out with him and Joe
   c) a date with Bond girl Lea Seydoux
   d) a trip home to see his family in South Africa

3. **What does roommate Joe find most annoying about living with Caspar?**
   a) he leaves mess everywhere
   b) he leaves the toilet seat up
   c) he punches him a lot
   d) he walks around naked all day

4. **What's the one thing that has made Caspar cry since he moved to London?**
   a) his girlfriend coming round to his apartment to break up with him
   b) Joe eating the last slice of pizza
   c) missing Christmas with his mum
   d) the brain freeze challenge

5. **Which part of his body does Caspar work on most?**
   a) his legs
   b) his chest
   c) his arms
   d) his bottom

6. **What has Caspar said is his greatest fear?**
   a) heights
   b) spiders
   c) Joe creeping round the house in the dark
   d) doing stand-up comedy in front of an audience

7. How old was Caspar when he had his first kiss?
    a) 13   **c)** 11
    b) 12   **d)** 18

8. What is Caspar's favourite day of the week?
    a) Saturday   **c)** Friday
    b) Tuesday   **d)** Sunday

9. What is Caspar's favourite nickname for himself?
    a) Cas   **c)** Caspar the Friendly Ghost
    b) Caspy   **d)** Cassie

10. How tall is Caspar?
    a) 6ft 2   **c)** 6ft
    b) 5ft 11   **d)** 6ft 1

11. What is Caspar's favourite type of music?
    a) dubstep   **c)** hip hop
    b) pop   **d)** rock

12. What subject does Caspar say he received the highest mark in at school?
    a) woodwork   **c)** maths
    b) geography   **d)** English

13. What part of Caspar and Joe's house does Caspar use as his office?
    a) the kitchen   **c)** the living room
    b) his bedroom   **d)** the dining room

14. What does Caspar miss most about school?
    a) watching a movie in class instead of   **c)** his favourite teacher
        having a proper lesson   **d)** school lunches
    b) his friends

15. What did Caspar get as a birthday present when he turned 18?
    a) a laptop   **c)** a TV
    b) a car   **d)** an iPhone

THE FUTURE IS BRIGHT

So what's next for vlogging superstar Caspar Lee? As well as being a hugely popular YouTuber around the world, he's also acting, has tried his hand at comedy, made a movie and even attempted singing, too. Could a bigger career in acting perhaps be next?

While Caspar has another movie on the horizon – *Laid in America,* co-starring fellow YouTuber KSI – in a 2015 video, he did promise his fans that he wouldn't leave YouTube as it is the thing he loves to do most. So expect to see lots more of Caspar's fun, hilarious videos as he travels the world, makes people laugh and annoys poor roommate Joe in any way he can. And we're sure that whatever Caspar chooses to do over the next few years, it's going to be really interesting... and broadcast on YouTube, of course!